FLY FISHING

BY BLAKE POUND

BELLWETHER MEDIA • MINNEAPOLIS, MN

Jump into the cockpit and take flight with Pilot books. Your journey will take you on high-energy adventures as you learn about all that is wild, weird, fascinating, and fun!

This edition first published in 2013 by Bellwether Media, Inc.

No part of this publication may be reproduced in whole or in part without written permission of the publisher. For information regarding permission, write to Bellwether Media, Inc., Attention: Permissions Department, 5357 Penn Avenue South, Minneapolis, MN 55419.

Library of Congress Cataloging-in-Publication Data

Pound, Blake.
 Fly fishing / by Blake Pound.
     p. cm. – (Pilot books: outdoor adventures)
 Includes bibliographical references and index.
 Summary: "Engaging images accompany information about fly fishing. The combination of high-interest subject matter and narrative text is intended for students in grades 3 through 7"–Provided by publisher.
 ISBN 978-1-60014-798-2 (hardcover : alk. paper)
 1. Fly fishing–Juvenile literature. I. Title.
 SH456.P67 2013   2012002387

Printed in the United States of America, North Mankato, MN.

TABLE OF CONTENTS

CASTING THE LINE

An **angler** wades in the water near the edge of a flowing river. She is careful to move slowly and remain very quiet. In her hand she holds a long, thin **fly rod**. The clear water reveals a school of brown trout just below the surface. The angler stands very still. She draws back the rod and flicks it forward. At the end of the line, a **fly** jumps back and forth over the water.

A small brown trout catches sight of the fly. It leaps out of the water to grab it. Caught by a small hook, the trout fights to get back into the river. It wriggles free and quickly swims away. The angler will have to try her luck with another fish.

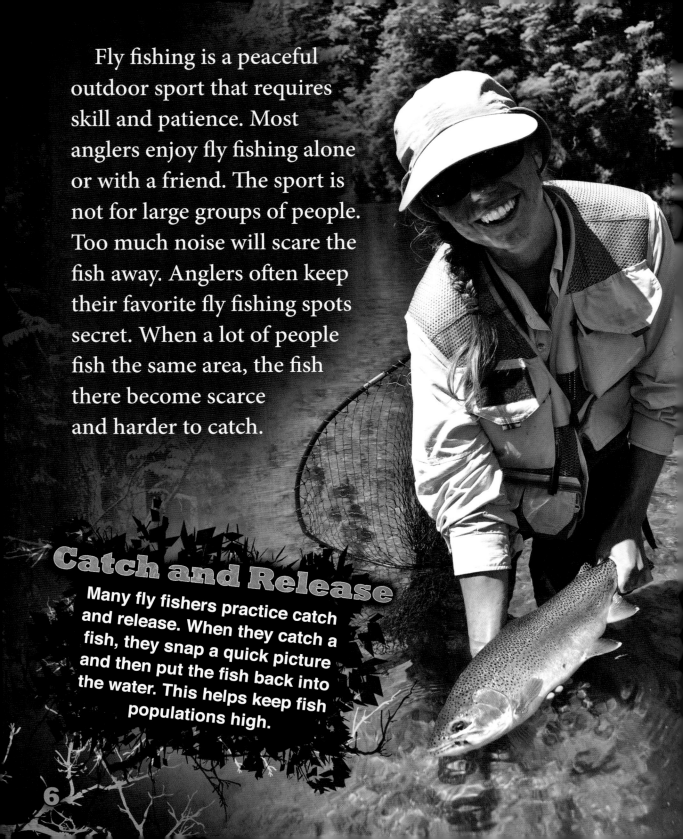

Fly fishing is a peaceful outdoor sport that requires skill and patience. Most anglers enjoy fly fishing alone or with a friend. The sport is not for large groups of people. Too much noise will scare the fish away. Anglers often keep their favorite fly fishing spots secret. When a lot of people fish the same area, the fish there become scarce and harder to catch.

Catch and Release

Many fly fishers practice catch and release. When they catch a fish, they snap a quick picture and then put the fish back into the water. This helps keep fish populations high.

Anglers have the best luck when fish are looking for food. Trout and other fish are most active when the weather is cool and the wind is blowing. Anglers know to head to their favorite river or lake in the early morning or evening.

Knowing how to **cast** is the key to successful fly fishing. Anglers use their hands to control the fly rod and the line coming out of the **reel**. The heavy line pulls a fly through the air, making it look like a bug flying in the wind. The angler lets the fly land on the water for a brief time. If no fish bite, the angler pulls the line out of the water and prepares for another cast. If a fish bites, the angler jerks the rod up quickly to **set the hook**.

Basic Casts

Standard ..... Used during normal conditions without obstacles

Point the rod toward the fishing area, and then draw it straight up and slightly behind you. When you feel the pull of the line, quickly cast it forward.

False .... Used to change the direction of the line between casts or to dry out a wet fly

Cast the line backward and forward, but don't let the fly land on the water.

Roll .... Used when there is no room to cast backward

Raise the rod tip until the line is slightly behind you. Whip the rod forward, but stop just before it is horizontal with the water. Let the line roll out in front of you.

Side .... Used in heavy winds or under low-hanging branches

Hold the rod to your right or left. Keep the rod horizontal as you draw it back. When you feel the pull of the line behind you, cast forward.

Haul .... Used to achieve distance and accuracy in windy conditions

Cast the rod forward with one hand, and tug lightly on the line near the reel with the other hand. This creates tension and increases the line's outward speed.

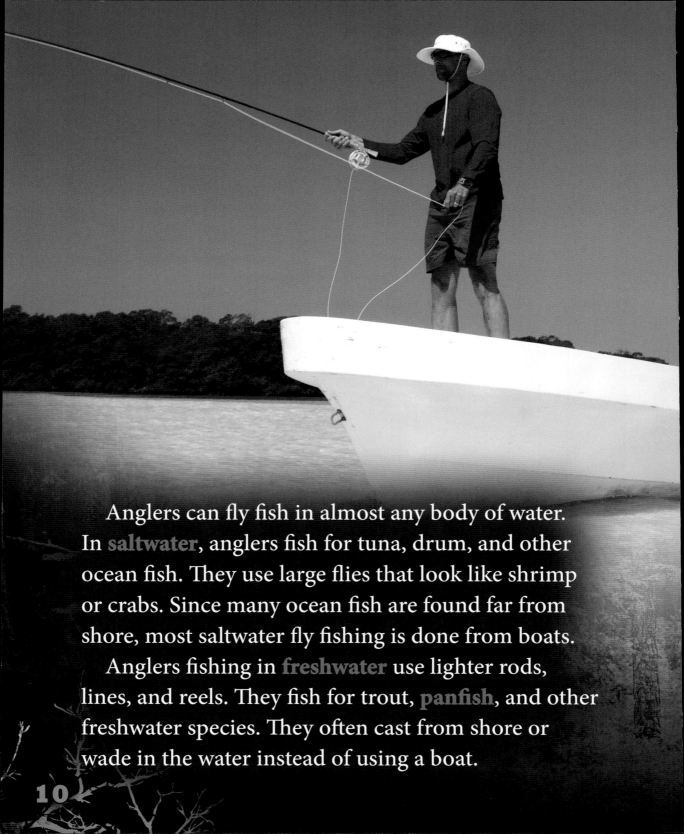

Anglers can fly fish in almost any body of water. In saltwater, anglers fish for tuna, drum, and other ocean fish. They use large flies that look like shrimp or crabs. Since many ocean fish are found far from shore, most saltwater fly fishing is done from boats.

Anglers fishing in freshwater use lighter rods, lines, and reels. They fish for trout, panfish, and other freshwater species. They often cast from shore or wade in the water instead of using a boat.

Off the Hook

Salmon and bass can be found in both freshwater and saltwater. They are a favorite of anglers because they are famous for putting up a fight!

salmon

FLY FISHING EQUIPMENT

Anglers need to gather a lot of fly fishing equipment before heading to their favorite stream. They bring fly rods instead of normal fishing poles. Fly rods are longer and more flexible for casting. They bend easier because they are especially thin and lightweight.

Fly anglers measure the weight of their rods on a scale of 1 to 15. The higher the number, the heavier and stronger the rod. Line weight should always match the rod weight. An angler might use a 3-weight rod to go after small trout. For larger fish such as drum, an angler would need an 8-weight or heavier.

Fly anglers use small nets to gather fish from the water. They bring baskets or buckets to store the fish they want to bring home. Waterproof boots and **waders** keep anglers dry if they are entering the water.

Anglers select flies with great care. Flies come in a variety of different sizes, colors, and designs. Many anglers also make their own flies. They spend hours tying together feathers, beads, and thread. Some even use their own hair! They try to make their flies look just like bugs or baitfish.

Flies can be wet or dry. A dry fly stays on the surface of the water. Fish must lunge upward to catch it. A wet fly sinks, sometimes all the way to the bottom. Anglers choose their flies based on the type of fish they are trying to catch.

flies

Barbless Is Best

Barbs are the small, sharp points that help keep fish on the hook. Many anglers who practice catch and release choose barbless hooks because they do less damage to the fish.

PLANNING AND RESPECT

Fly fishing takes careful planning. Anglers often travel a long way for a rewarding fishing experience. Before they head out, they study maps and talk with people who know the bodies of water. They also purchase a **license** from each state where they plan to fish. Anglers who want to fish on private land need to get permission from the owner.

Anglers should **scout** the waters for spots where fish gather and feed. Experienced anglers look for fallen trees, rocky bottoms, and other places where fish like to hide. Anglers should also pay attention to the weather. Fish are less active on hot days. On windy days, fish gather to feed on bugs that are blown over the water. Sunny days make it easier to spot fish under the surface.

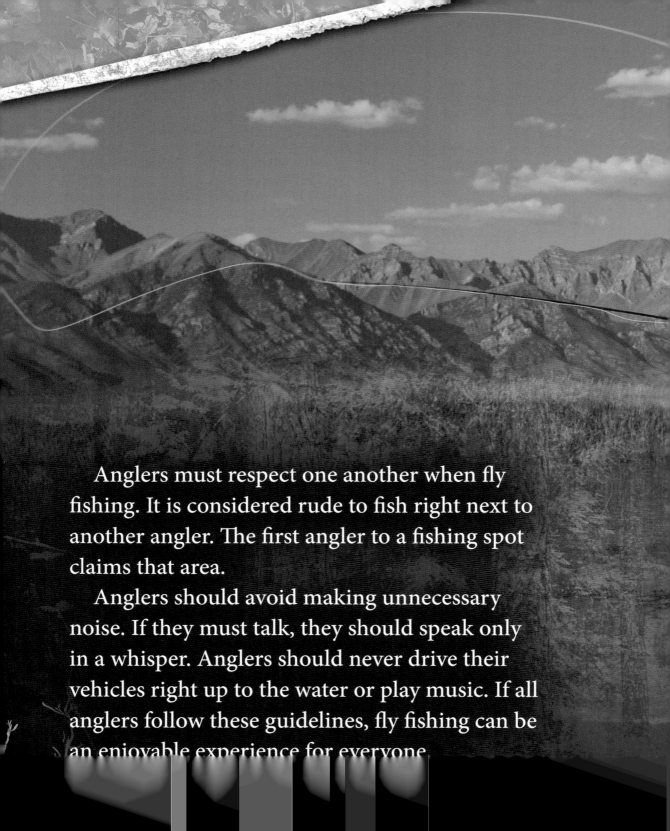

Anglers must respect one another when fly fishing. It is considered rude to fish right next to another angler. The first angler to a fishing spot claims that area.

Anglers should avoid making unnecessary noise. If they must talk, they should speak only in a whisper. Anglers should never drive their vehicles right up to the water or play music. If all anglers follow these guidelines, fly fishing can be an enjoyable experience for everyone.

FISHING THE GREEN RIVER

The Green River flows through steep canyons in Utah. Downstream from the Flaming Gorge Dam, the water forms deep pools between walls of red rock. Anglers come here for rainbow and brown trout. It is easy to spot the fish as they dart through the crystal clear water. Anglers can cast from shore or float in a small boat on the river.

Guides take anglers to the best spots on the Green River. Dirt roads bring them to small boat ramps. Hiking trails lead them farther into the wilderness for a day of **remote** fly fishing. At several points, small beaches line the river shore. Anglers can sit, talk, and fry up the catch of the day.

GLOSSARY

angler—a person who fishes

baitfish—small fish that attract game fish

cast—to work the fly rod and line in order to move a fly over the water

dam—a large structure built to control the flow of a river

fly—a fishhook covered in feathers, hair, or other materials to make it look like a bug or baitfish

fly rod—a fishing pole used by fly anglers

freshwater—water with little to no salt; lakes, ponds, rivers, and streams contain freshwater.

guides—professional anglers who instruct other anglers on where, when, and how to catch fish

license—a document that gives legal permission to do an activity

panfish—fish that are small enough to fry in a pan; sunfish, crappies, and bluegills are types of panfish.

reel—a device that allows an angler to pull in and let out fishing line

remote—far removed from human development

saltwater—water with a high amount of salt

scout—to explore an area to learn more about it

set the hook—to firmly secure a hook in a fish's mouth by jerking the fly rod

waders—waterproof pants that cover anglers from their feet to their waists

TO LEARN MORE

At the Library

Befus, Tyler. *A Kid's Guide to Flyfishing: It's More than Catching Fish.* Boulder, Colo.: Johnson Books, 2007.

Jenson-Elliott, Cynthia L. *Fly Fishing.* Mankato, Minn.: Capstone Press, 2012.

Kleinkauf, Cecilia. *River Girls: Fly Fishing for Young Women.* Boulder, Colo.: Johnson Books, 2006.

On the Web

Learning more about fly fishing is as easy as 1, 2, 3.

1. Go to www.factsurfer.com.

2. Enter "fly fishing" into the search box.

3. Click the "Surf" button and you will see a list of related Web sites.

With factsurfer.com, finding more information is just a click away.

INDEX